A Mob of
Meerkats
and Other Mammal Groups

Louise Spilsbury

Heinemann
LIBRARY
Chicago, Illinois

www.capstonepub.com
Visit our website to find out more information about Heinemann-Raintree books.

To order:
☎ Phone 800-747-4992
💻 Visit www.capstonepub.com to browse our catalog and order online.

Edited by Nancy Dickmann, Adam Miller, and Laura Knowles
Designed by Richard Parker
Original illustrations © Capstone Global Library Ltd 2013
Illustrations by Jeff Edwards
Picture research by Ruth Blair

Originated by Capstone Global Library Ltd
Printed and bound in China by CTPS

16 15 14 13 12
10 9 8 7 6 5 4 3 2 1

Library of Congress Cataloging-in-Publication Data
Spilsbury, Louise.
  A mob of meerkats, and other mammal groups / Louise Spilsbury.
       p. cm.—(Animals in groups)
  Includes bibliographical references and index.
  ISBN 978-1-4329-6481-8 (hb)—ISBN 978-1-4329-6488-7 (pb) 1. Meerkat—Juvenile literature. 2. Mammals—Juvenile literature. I. Title.
  QL737.C235S67 2013
  599.74′2—dc23   2011038137

Acknowledgments
We would like to thank the following for permission to reproduce photographs: Alamy pp. 20 (© Ann and Steve Toon), 25 (© Adam Seward), 27 (© David Crausby); Corbis p. 29 (© Paul A. Souders); FLPA pp. 9 (Vincent Grafhorst/Minden Pictures), 19 (ImageBroker/Imagebroker), iStockphoto pp. 10 (© Jesse Smith), 24 (© Neal McClimon), 33 (© Peter Malsbury); Naturepl pp. 7 (© Solvin Zankl), 15, 21 (© Simon King), 30 (© RICHARD DU TOIT), 31 (© David Curl), 32 (© Charlie Summers), 41 (© Marguerite Smits Van Oyen); Photolibrary pp. 13, 14 (David Macdonald/OSF); Science Photo Library p. 39 (NEIL BROMHALL); Shutterstock p. 4 (© mroz), 5 (© AnetaPics), 8 (© Photodynamic), 11 (© Gert Johannes Jacobus Very), 16 (© EcoPrint), 23 (© niall dunne), 28 (© Henk Bentlage), 35 (© Ewan Chesser), 37 (© Villiers Steyn).

Cover photograph of Suricate or meerkat (*Suricata suricatta*) males looking for enemies reproduced with permission of Shutterstock (© Aaljana).

Every effort has been made to contact copyright holders of any material reproduced in this book. Any omissions will be rectified in subsequent printings if notice is given to the publisher.

Disclaimer
All the Internet addresses (URLs) given in this book were valid at the time of going to press. However, due to the dynamic nature of the Internet, some addresses may have changed, or sites may have changed or ceased to exist since publication. While the author and publisher regret any inconvenience this may cause readers, no responsibility for any such changes can be accepted by either the author or the publisher.

Contents

DID YOU KNOW?

Discover amazing facts about meerkats.

HUMAN INTERACTION

Find out what happens when humans and meerkats come into contact with each other.

HABITAT IN DANGER

Learn how meerkats' habitats are under threat, and what is being done to protect them.

Some words are shown in bold, **like this**. You can find out what they mean by looking in the glossary.

Welcome to the Mob!

Meerkats are only about the size of a squirrel, but they are some of Africa's most famous animals! You would probably recognize them right away. They have gray-brown fur with dark stripes across their backs. They have a long, pointed nose and mouth, called a snout, and small, rounded black ears. Meerkats look like they are wearing goggles, because their small eyes have a circle of black fur around them! They also have a long, stiff tail that they use to help them balance when they stand up with their front paws in the air.

Meerkats are not cats at all! They are a kind of mongoose, a group of long-bodied **mammals** that live mainly in Africa.

Meerkat mobs

The fact that meerkats are small animals means there are lots of larger animals that try to eat them. In order to survive, meerkats live in groups. A group of meerkats is called a mob or a gang. Some mobs have only five meerkats, but in other mobs there may be thirty or more animals. Mobs of meerkats live and feed together. They share jobs like watching out for **predators** and caring for young meerkats.

Can you count the members in this meerkat mob?

Where Do Meerkats Live?

Meerkats live in southern Africa, in countries such as South Africa, Botswana, Mozambique, and Zimbabwe. Meerkats live in flat, dry parts of these countries, and many meerkats live in parts of the Kalahari **Desert**, one of the biggest deserts in the world.

Hot and dry

In this part of the world, it is very hot and dry. In the summer months, high temperatures make the sand feel burning hot. When temperatures drop at night, it can get very cold. The region gets some rain, but not enough for many plants or trees to grow. Mostly grasses and low plants grow in the sand and among the rocks.

Meerkats in their habitat

Animals have features that help them to live in their **habitat**. The meerkat's gray-brown fur and striped back is a kind of **camouflage**. It helps meerkats to blend in with the sandy soils and dry plants where they live. Their color makes it harder for predators to see them against the sand. Some experts think the black tip on the end of their tail helps meerkats, too. When they hold up their tail, other members of the mob can see them, even in long grass.

Did you know?

The black patches of fur around a meerkat's eyes work in a similar way to sunglasses. They reduce the glare from the bright desert sunlight, to help meerkats see more clearly.

The place where an animal lives is called its habitat. Meerkats live on open plains, like this one.

Meerkats in the morning

The weather in the meerkats' habitat affects everything they do during the day. Desert nights can be very cold, so meerkats sleep together inside their **burrows**. The first thing meerkats do in the morning is warm up in the sun. Animals in the mob stand together on their back legs, with their stomachs tilted toward the sky.

DID YOU KNOW?

There is a patch on a meerkat's stomach where the hair is quite thin and the black skin beneath shows through. Dark colors take in heat, so meerkats use this patch of dark skin to collect heat and warm up on cool mornings.

This family of meerkats is warming up in the morning sun.

Hiding from the heat

Meerkats feed in the morning, but by midday it becomes too hot to be in the sun, so meerkats rest in the shade of plants. Sometimes they go into their burrows for an afternoon nap. Meerkat burrows measure up to 16 feet (5 meters) across, and they are about 5 feet (1.5 meters) below the ground. The temperature stays the same deep under the ground.

These meerkat pups are taking shelter in their burrow, out of the hot afternoon sun.

HABITAT IN DANGER

Climate change is likely to cause hotter weather and faster winds in the Kalahari. This could blow whole sand dunes over desert plants. This would rob meerkats of shade and food.

Sandy shelters

When it is cooler in the evening, meerkat mobs often work together on their burrows. They use their sharp, curved claws like shovels to dig tunnels and rooms into the sandy soils where they live. Each network of burrows has many entrances, so the meerkats can get in and out of it quickly and easily. Each mob may have five or more burrows, and meerkats move around to different burrows every couple of days.

Meerkats can close their small ears to keep the sand out when they are digging!

DID YOU KNOW?

A mob of meerkats builds all of its burrows within an area of land about 0.4 to 1.2 square miles (1 to 3 square kilometers), depending on the size of the group. This is called its **territory**.

Yellow mongooses are closely related to meerkats and often share the same burrow.

Sharing the habitat

Meerkats share their burrows with other animals. Meerkats usually dig their own burrows, but sometimes they move into burrows dug by ground squirrels or yellow mongooses. The animals live together and share the job of taking care of the burrow. They also help each other to spot predators! A variety of beetles also move into meerkat burrows. Dung beetles roll meerkat dung (solid waste) out of the burrows. They save the dung to eat later or they lay their eggs in it.

HABITAT IN DANGER

Climate change means hotter, drier weather, which makes it hard for plants to grow. Meerkat burrows help the habitat. Water and seeds collect in the upper tunnels, helping new plants to grow.

How Do Meerkat Mobs Feed?

A meerkat mob hunts for food in a different part of its territory each day. The mob spreads out, and each meerkat uses its good sense of smell to sniff around in search of **prey**. Meerkats mostly feed on insects, spiders, and millipedes. They also eat small lizards, **rodents**, and sometimes scorpions and birds. If one meerkat finds a large prey item, such as a lizard, other meerkats may share the job of catching and eating it.

HUMAN INTERACTION

Meerkats feed for 5 to 8 hours a day, and 80 percent of their diet is insects. They help people by eating many of the insects that damage or eat farmers' crops.

Digging for dinner

Meerkats find most of their food under the ground. As soon as they smell it, they start to dig with their curved claws. They have to dig as fast as they can, before their prey gets away. Meerkats dig hundreds of holes every morning in their search for food. Their job is even harder in summer, because insects crawl deeper underground to escape the heat.

DID YOU KNOW?

Meerkats have a thin layer of skin between the surface of the eye and eyelid called a **nictitating membrane**, which wipes sand from their eyes every time they blink.

A meerkat often has to dig its own body weight in sand or soil to get just one small insect!

A dangerous dinner?

Some scorpions can kill other animals and even people with **venom** from the stinger at the end of their tail. Yet meerkats eat scorpions. A meerkat grabs a scorpion with its front paws, bites off the stinger, and spits it out. It then drags the scorpion across the sand. This rubs off any venom on the surface of the scorpion's body.

HUMAN INTERACTION

Meerkats are such good hunters that in parts of southern Africa some people catch them, keep them in cages, and use them to kill rodents in their homes. Animal welfare groups say keeping meerkats alone like this makes them unhappy and sick.

Meerkats are immune to some scorpion venom, which means the stings cannot hurt them. But they still handle all scorpions very carefully.

Meerkats and water

The word *meerkat* means "lake cat" or "marsh cat" in a South African language—but meerkats are not cats, and they do not really like water! They usually run into their dry burrows when it rains. They will drink from pools of water that form during the rainy season, but meerkats get almost all the water they need from their food.

Meerkats get some water by digging up and eating plant roots that contain water.

HABITAT IN DANGER

In periods of very dry weather, water dries up completely. Then most of the plants in the habitat die and meerkats can die, too. In 1995, the number of meerkats in the Kalahari dropped by almost two-thirds after a very long period without rain.

Guard duty

When meerkats feed, they cannot watch for predators. So, they take turns looking out for danger. One or two meerkats stand on a mound of earth or go up a tree to watch for predators. After about an hour, other meerkats take over guard duty. If a guard meerkat spots danger, it makes a loud barking sound. Then the members of the mob run into their burrows as fast as they can.

Meerkats have good long-distance eyesight, so guards can spot predators from far away.

DID YOU KNOW?

Meerkat burrows have many special tunnels with wide openings, so lots of meerkats can run into them at the same time. Meerkats have more than 1,000 **bolt holes** in their territory, so they can go to one right away if danger comes.

Meerkat predators

Meerkat guards are on the lookout for their main predators. Birds of prey, such as eagles and hawks, hunt them from the air. On the ground, meerkats are hunted by jackals (a type of wild dog), wild cats, and large snakes. The meerkats run into burrows to escape birds, but they group together to chase off land predators. The mob moves toward a predator, hissing and growling. They fool the predator into thinking they are one large and fierce animal! When a group of smaller animals chase off a bigger enemy like this, it is called mobbing.

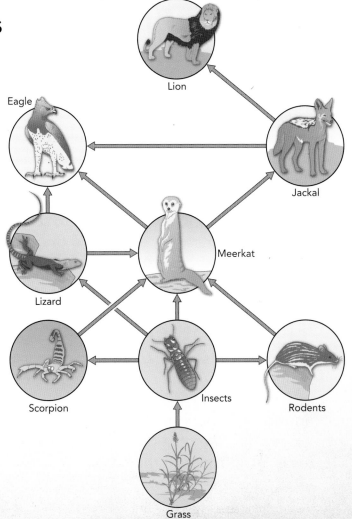

Lion

Eagle

Jackal

Lizard

Meerkat

Scorpion

Insects

Rodents

Grass

Meerkats are an important part of the food web where they live. Arrows point from each living thing to an animal that eats it.

HUMAN INTERACTION

Meerkat guards watch for animal predators, but humans can also be a danger. In some places, people have killed meerkats because they can carry a disease called rabies, which they can pass to humans.

Who's Who in a Meerkat Mob?

One female meerkat and one male meerkat are the leaders of a mob. They are known as the **alpha** male and the alpha female. The alpha female is the real boss, and she often chooses which meerkat becomes the alpha male. The alpha pair chooses which direction to go searching for food in the morning and when to move to another burrow. The rest of the adult meerkats in the mob help to take care of the young, dig tunnels and burrows, and guard the group. All of the meerkats in a mob know how to do these different jobs, so everyone takes turns doing them.

Fighting other mobs

If a mob spots another gang of meerkats in its territory, the alpha pair leads their mob in a kind of war dance. All the meerkats hold their tails in the air and run and jump toward the intruders, shouting and pawing the ground. If the war dance does not scare off a rival gang, meerkats will bite, scratch, and even kill intruders if they can.

HABITAT IN DANGER

People are taking over more and more areas of wild habitat for farms, homes, and other buildings. In some places, roads have been built across or through meerkat territories. Some meerkats are accidentally killed by cars when they have to cross the roads.

A meerkat mob's war dance is usually enough to scare another mob away.

Staying on top

In a small mob, the alpha pair are the parents of all the other meerkats in the group. Larger mobs are made up of several different family groups. In these big mobs, the alpha pair still has most of the babies, but other meerkats may **breed** as well. The alpha pair can stay in charge of a mob for several years—unless they get killed by a predator. After several years, a younger meerkat from inside their mob or from another mob may fight them and take their place.

An alpha female may kill other females' young so that the females help care for her pups instead, giving them a better chance of survival.

Moving mobs

When meerkats are about a year old, they are fully grown. By two or three years old, many young male meerkats have left their parents' mob. Males often leave in groups of two or three to start new mobs or join other mobs. Sometimes a young male fights the alpha male in his own or another mob, to try to take over as boss.

Adult females do not usually choose to leave their mob. They are chased out by the alpha female when it is time for her to give birth. One reason for this is to stop them from taking over as boss while she is weak. Most of these females return to the group later, but some form new mobs with unrelated males.

It is normal for the alpha female to chase off the other female meerkats before she gives birth.

How Do Meerkats Communicate?

Meerkats communicate in several different ways: sounds, **body language**, and scent. Communication allows meerkats to share information, keeps them safe, and helps them to feel like a team.

Talk about it!

Meerkats make a lot of different sounds. The alpha pair gives one kind of call that tells the mob to follow when it is time to find food. Meerkats can spread out up to 16 feet (5 meters) apart when feeding and are often hidden in the grass. So, they constantly make soft growling sounds to tell one another where they are. Meerkat guards also repeat a sound to tell the rest of the mob that all is clear.

DID YOU KNOW?

Although meerkats are not cats, they do make a purring sound when they feel safe and content.

Meerkat guards use different calls to alert the mob to different dangers. If a meerkat sees something suspicious, it makes a sound that tells the rest of the mob to be prepared. The other meerkats may stop and look up. If the guard sees a real threat, it gives a sharp, shrill call. This tells the mob to run for cover. Meerkat guards make different types of sounds to tell the mob whether the predator is on land or in the air. When the predator gets too close for comfort, the guard runs for cover, too.

A guard meerkat's alarm calls are noisiest and fastest when a predator is very close and very dangerous!

Body language

Meerkats also use body language to communicate. For example, when a meerkat guard sounds the alarm, it turns its body and stares in the direction of the predator. This tells other meerkats in the mob where the threat is coming from.

Scent marking

Meerkats urinate (release liquid waste) regularly around the edge of their territory. This marks it with the mob's smell. Meerkats also have a scent pouch below their tail. These pouches release a scented fluid when meerkats rub against rocks and plants. When meerkats mark their territory with scent, it is like putting an invisible fence around the land. It tells other mobs where their territory is and to keep out.

Other meerkats usually move away from a mob's territory when they smell the scent markings. If they do not move away, fights can break out.

Grooming and licking

Meerkats **groom** each other by picking tiny insects and dirt out of each other's fur with their claws and teeth. This keeps the mob clean, but it also helps to make meerkats feel closer to each other. Meerkats also lick each other's faces, especially when they meet up after being apart. Grooming and licking each other makes meerkats in a mob smell alike because of the scent in their saliva (spit). This helps meerkats to recognize each other, because their eyesight is not very good close-up.

Grooming and licking each other is an important part of meerkat daily life.

HUMAN INTERACTION

Meerkats have helped farmers understand how a disease called tuberculosis (TB) passes among cattle. Scientists studying meerkats found that they catch TB by grooming and licking each other.

How Do Meerkats Care for Their Young?

Meerkats are mammals, so they give birth to live young. A female meerkat can have up to four **litters** of three to eight babies every year. Meerkat babies are called pups. When meerkat pups are first born, they do not have their full coat of hair and their eyes and ears are closed. They are totally helpless for about 10 days. They mostly sleep and **suckle** milk from their mother's body.

Baby burrows

Most meerkat pups are born during the warmer, wetter part of the year between October and April. This is when there is the most food available. The mob stays in the burrow the pups were born in for three weeks, until the pups can leave it.

Babysitters

All the adult meerkats in a mob take turns to guard the burrow from predators while the pups are in there. These babysitters may stay on guard all day while the alpha female is away feeding. She needs to keep eating so that she can produce milk for the pups. The babysitters also watch the weather. If heavy rains fall, the burrow can flood. Adults carry the young to safety, to a higher room in the burrow or to high ground.

DID YOU KNOW?

Other female adult meerkats can suckle the pups, even if they have never been pregnant. This allows them to provide the pups with milk while their mother is away.

Meerkat pups weigh about 1 ounce (30 grams) at birth. That is the same as a small bag of chips! These pups are just a few weeks old.

Leaving the burrow

When baby meerkats first start to spend the daytime outside, they stay close to the burrow. They continue suckling milk until they are about two months old, but they also begin to try insects and other kinds of food. They follow the meerkats who are searching for food and squeak constantly to get the adults' attention. The pups that cry and beg loudest get the most food!

DID YOU KNOW?

Only one in four meerkat pups makes it to adulthood. Many pups are killed by predators. Others are killed by adult females who want their own pups to have a better chance of survival. Some pups die when burrows flood with rain.

Meerkat pups take their first wobbly steps out from the dark, safe burrow into the sun at about three weeks old.

Protecting the pups

Whether the pups are outside or inside the burrow, there are always adult meerkats around to watch over them. If the pups are outside and a guard meerkat gives an alarm call, babysitters carry them into the burrow. If there is no time to get inside, adults protect the young by crouching over them. Adults also gang together to attack predators that try to get the young or follow the pups into the burrow.

Adult meerkats carry pups by the scruff of the neck.

HUMAN INTERACTION

Predators are not the only danger to pups. People have stolen some pups from their mobs and sold them as pets. Meerkats do not make good pets. They dig constantly and can become aggressive and bite other pets and their owners.

Time for school!

Many young animals learn only by watching adults, but adult meerkats actually teach the pups! Each pup has an adult meerkat that acts as its teacher. Male meerkats usually teach male pups, while females teach female pups. The adult meerkats teach pups how to hunt, what food to eat, and which animals could be dangerous.

Pups learn some things by watching the adults, such as how to dig. But adult meerkats also teach pups what to do.

DID YOU KNOW?

Adult meerkats care for the pups for the sake of the mob. In large mobs, there are more meerkats to fight rival mobs over territory. There are also more eyes to look out for predators.

Learning to hunt

When pups are very young, adults bring them dead prey to eat. Adult meerkats start teaching pups how to hunt when the pups are about six weeks old. At this point, adults bring them live prey, so they can practice how to catch and kill it. Sometimes an adult runs with prey in its mouth until a pup manages to snatch it away from them! Or an adult pushes a prey animal toward the pup to show the pup that it is good to eat. Adults also remove a live scorpion's stinger before giving it to the pups. This gives the pups a chance to learn how to handle difficult prey without getting hurt or killed.

An adult member of the mob has brought this pup a lizard to help it practice its hunting skills.

Playtime

Adult meerkats also watch over the pups while they play, and they sometimes join in the games, too. When pups play, at least one meerkat stands guard to keep them safe. Meerkats are curious animals, and pups can make a toy of almost anything they find, from twigs and pebbles to empty snail shells. Some people claim to have even seen meerkats competing against each other in races! Meerkat pups also spend a lot of time play-fighting. They wrestle, stand up and grab each other by the shoulders, and push and shove. They leap out onto each other, pin each other down, and bite and gnaw at each other's ears and legs!

Young meerkat pups spend much of the daytime playing.

Why do pups play?

Scientists are not exactly sure why meerkat pups play and fight like this. They may do it for a number of reasons. One reason might be that fighting teaches them skills that will help them fight off attacks by other mobs when they are older. Another idea is that playing strengthens the **bonds** between members of the meerkat mob, just like playing together makes members of a team feel closer. One reason the pups play and fight might be just because it is fun!

Young meerkats get fit, learn fighting skills, and bond with other members of the mob when they play-fight.

DID YOU KNOW?

Meerkat pups make a soft sound when they are playing, which gets louder and faster when they are excited or fighting.

Do Other African Mammals Live in Groups?

Several other types of African mammal live in groups. Most lions live in groups called prides in hot, dry **savannah** habitats. There can be fifteen to forty lions in a single pride, including two or three males, some females, and their young. Unlike meerkats, the adult males are the leaders of a pride. Males patrol the territory and mark it with urine (liquid waste) and scratch marks to warn other lions to keep out. They attack intruders that enter the territory. Females do most of the hunting for the pride and take care of the cubs.

Living together

No predators attack a healthy pride of lions. The pride's only threat comes from other prides of lions. Lions hunt together to catch large prey such as zebra or buffalo, so the pride only has to feed every two or three days. Lions also live together to care for the cubs. Lionesses can suckle each other's cubs and watch over them while the mother is away feeding or hunting.

HABITAT IN DANGER

Wild lions once lived all over Africa, but the spread of humans has forced them to live in smaller areas. Humans take over savannah habitats to build farms and towns. This means there are fewer areas of grass to eat and therefore fewer grazing animals such as zebras. This in turn means fewer lions, because there is less food for them to eat.

Like meerkats, lions communicate using sound. Lionesses grunt to keep in touch with one another while hunting.

Elephant herds

Most elephants live in **herds** of six to twelve individuals, but herds can be bigger. The herd is led by the oldest female, who can be up to 60 years old. As in meerkat mobs, the alpha female decides when to move and where to stop to feed. Unlike meerkats, the rest of the herd is made up of the alpha female's sisters, adult daughters, and their young. All males leave their mother's herd when they are 12 or 13. Males roam around alone or in small groups together.

Caring for the young

Groups of male and female elephants only come together when it is time to breed. Males and females do not stay together after that, which means male elephants do not help to raise the herd's young. Female herd members help each other take care of and protect the baby elephants, which are called calves.

An elephant calf can suckle from other females in the herd as well as its mother. If a predator or an unfamiliar elephant approaches the herd, the elephants form a circle around the calves and roar angrily to protect the young. As in meerkat mobs, older elephants in a herd teach younger ones the things they need to know to survive, such as what food to eat and where to find it.

DID YOU KNOW?

The African elephant is the largest land animal in the world. An adult can weigh as much as four cars!

African elephants live in forest or savannah habitats across different parts of Africa.

Naked mole rats

Naked mole rats look like saber-toothed sausages with their pink, almost hairless bodies and enormous front teeth! Like meerkats, they live in large groups and dig underground burrows. They use their big teeth to dig and to eat underground plant parts, which also contain water. As in meerkat mobs, one female is larger than the others and has the babies. Other mole rats care for the babies, find food, and look after and defend the burrow from other mole rats and predators such as snakes.

HUMAN INTERACTION

Naked mole rat colonies sometimes destroy whole fields of crops by eating all the plant roots.

Group life

One reason naked mole rats live in groups is that they can dig faster to find food if they work together. They line up nose to tail along a tunnel and the mole rat at the front uses its teeth to break through new soil. Mole rats behind them use their feet like brooms to sweep soil backward, while other mole rats kick soil up to the surface. Unlike most other mammals, naked mole rats cannot maintain a steady body temperature, so they huddle in groups for warmth. Naked mole rats, like meerkats, recognize each other by smell. But they create a shared scent by rolling in the burrow's toilet chamber!

DID YOU KNOW?

An underground colony of about 80 naked mole rats can cover an area the size of about 10 football fields!

Naked mole rat groups are called colonies. Most have 80 to 100 members, but some have 300! Naked mole rats are found only in parts of Kenya, Ethiopia, and Somalia.

What's the Future for Meerkats?

Living in a mob is important to meerkats, just as being part of a family, school, or club is important to you. Animals may live together in order to protect their young. Predators always try to catch young or sick animals first, because they are weaker and cannot run as fast as healthy adults. Meerkats and naked mole rats also live in groups to share the work of digging and maintaining the burrows they need to survive in the hot, dry plains. These jobs would take too long and take up too much energy for one animal alone. Without the rest of its mob, a meerkat could not survive.

Conservation

Unlike some African mammals, such as lions, meerkats are not a threatened or **endangered species**. That means there is no immediate danger of the meerkat dying out. However, their habitat is being lost to buildings, and hot, dry weather causes habitat erosion, which is when the top layer of soil blows away from the land. Without this layer of soil, there are fewer plants. Fewer plants means fewer insects that feed on the plants, and that means fewer insects for meerkats to eat. Some governments have created national parks and reserves to keep land safe for meerkats and other animals.

HUMAN INTERACTION

The Kgalagadi Transfrontier National Park in the Kalahari Desert is several parks in different countries linked together to make one of the world's largest **conservation** areas. It protects meerkats and other mammals and birds.

Some national parks charge visitors to watch meerkats. They use the money to protect and maintain the land in the park.

Fact File

Size

Naked mole rats are about 3 inches (7 centimeters) long, meerkats are about 12 inches (30 centimeters) long, male lions grow up to 11.5 feet (3.5 meters) long, and male African elephants can grow up to about 25 feet (7.5 meters) long!

Life span

Lions and meerkats can live to about 10 years old in the wild. Naked mole rats are some of the longest-living members of the rodent family, usually living for between 10 and 30 years. Elephants can live to about 60 years old in the wild.

Teeth

Lions and meerkats have sharp, pointed teeth for grabbing prey and biting into it. A quarter of all the muscles in a naked mole rat's body are in its jaws, to help it use the four powerful teeth that extend outside its lips to bite through roots and to dig. African elephants use their trunks to put food into their mouths and have large molars (flat-topped back teeth) to crush and chew it. An elephant's tusks are special long teeth that it uses to scrape bark off trees to eat.

BIG BURROWS

Meerkats live in a large territory that has about 20 different sleeping burrows in it, each of which usually has several entrances. Some naked mole rat tunnel systems can be more than 2 miles (3 kilometers) long!

DEFENSE TACTICS

When threatened, meerkats may dig very quickly to create a cloud of dust that distracts their attacker and gives them time to get away. If snakes try to get into a naked mole rat burrow, the animals dig quickly and block the entrance with dirt. If that fails, a mole rat will attack the snake with its teeth, sometimes sacrificing its own life while others escape.

This map shows where meerkats live in Africa.

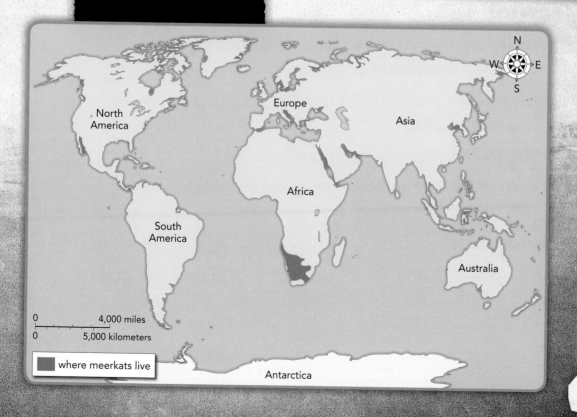

N
W E
S

North America

Europe

Asia

Africa

South America

Australia

Antarctica

0   4,000 miles
0   5,000 kilometers

☐ where meerkats live

Glossary

alpha name for the leading male or female in a pack

body language way of communicating using body posture, gestures, facial expressions, and eye movements, instead of sounds

bolt hole hole that an animal runs into to escape from predators

bond feeling of closeness with another animal

breed produce young

burrow hole or tunnel dug by an animal for shelter

camouflage colors and patterns that help an animal's body blend in with its background

climate change changes in the world's weather patterns caused by human activity

conservation protecting wildlife or places, and trying to save them from harm or damage

desert large area of land in a hot, dry region where few plants grow

endangered at risk of dying out

groom when an animal licks or cleans the hair and skin of another animal

habitat natural home or surroundings of a living thing

herd group of animals of the same type that live and feed together

litter set of young all born at the same time to the same parents

mammal hairy animal that feeds its young with milk from the mother's body

nictitating membrane clear inner eyelid in some animals that closes to protect and moisten the eye

predator animal that hunts and eats other animals

prey animal that is hunted and eaten by another animal

rodent mammal that has long incisor teeth that grow throughout its life

savannah large, open plain mostly covered in grasses and shrubs, with patches of trees

species particular type of living thing

suckle feed a baby mammal on milk from its mother's body

territory area of land that an animal marks out and guards as its own

venom poisonous liquid that some animals produce when they bite or sting

Find Out More

Books

Ganeri, Anita. *Meerkat* (A Day in the Life: Desert
    Animals). Chicago: Heinemann Library, 2011.
Newland, Sonya. *Desert Animals* (Saving Wildlife).
    Mankato, Minn.: Smart Apple Media, 2012.
Shalev, Zahavit. *Water Hole* (24 Hours). New York:
    Dorling Kindersley, 2005.
Silverman, Buffy. *Desert Food Chains* (Protecting Food
    Chains). Chicago: Heinemann Library, 2011.
Walden, Katherine. *Meerkats* (Safari Animals).
    New York: PowerKids, 2009.

Web sites

animal.discovery.com/fansites/meerkat/
    meerkat.html
Visit the web site of the television series *Meerkat
Manor* to see videos, play games, and read facts
about meerkats.

www.desertanimals.net
Find out about other desert animals at this web site.

kids.nationalgeographic.com/kids/animals/
    creaturefeature/meerkat
There are lots of meerkat pictures and facts on the
National Geographic web site.

DVDs

Meerkat Manor (seasons 1–4) (Discovery
   Communications, 2007–2009)

Places to visit

You can see meerkats in lots of zoos today. Try the San
Diego Zoo in California, the Smithsonian National Zoo
in Washington, D.C., the Fort Worth Zoo in Texas, or
the Brookfield Zoo in Illinois. You could also check the
Internet or use resources at your local library to find a
meerkat near you!

More topics to research

What did you enjoy finding out about most in this
book? Meerkats spend most of their time together,
and their ability to work and feed together helps
them to survive in their hot, open habitat. Perhaps
you could discover more about the meerkats' way of
life or research young meerkats and how they learn?
Or perhaps you would like to know more about the
different sounds they make to communicate? See if
you can find out more information in books at your
local library or on the Internet.

Index